5445 5406

LET'S MAKE A DIFFERENCE:

WE CAN HELP PROTECT
MOUNTAIN GORILLAS

Gabriella Francine
with Solara Vayanian

Illustrations by Phil Velikan

BBM BOOKS

Newport Beach, CA

We Can Help Protect Mountain Gorillas ©2013 Gabriella Francine

Library of Congress Control Number: 2013940230

Layout, cover and illustrations by Phil Velikan www.findphil.com
Editorial assistance provided by Dorothy Chambers
Packaged by Wish Publishing

Printed in China
10 9 8 7 6 5 4 3 2 1

Published by BBM Books

Photography credits

Cover image: © Photo courtesy of Jessica S. Burbridge, Gorilla Doctors
Title page: © szefei/shutterstock
Page 3: Ruth Keesling photo courtesy of Frank Keesling, background image © Helder Almeida/shutterstock
Page 4: © Andrew Molinaro/shutterstock
Page 5: background image © Andrii Muzyka/shutterstock, planet earth © Marcel Clemens/shutterstock
Page 6: © PRILL/shutterstock
Page 7: © erwinf/shutterstock
Page 8: © Andrew Molinaro/shutterstock
Page 9: © archideaphoto/shutterstock
Page 10: © FAUP/shutterstock
Page 11: © Joe Gough/shutterstock
Page 12: © PRILL/shutterstock
Page 13: © Artazum/shutterstock
Page 14: © Alberto Loyo/shutterstock

Page 15: bark © Vitaly Titov and Maria Sidelnikova/shutterstock, worm © motorolka/shutterstock, blackberries © Evgeny Karandaev, bugs © Pan Xunbin; leaves © Lim Yong Hian, jack fruit © ahnhuynh, wild celery © mtsyri
Page 16: © Ipics/shutterstock
Page 17: background © hkeita/shutterstock, Grauer's Gorilla Nest photo courtesy of Jessica S. Burbridge, Gorilla Doctors
Page 18: Photo courtesy of Jessica S. Burbridge, Gorilla Doctors
Page 20: Photo courtesy of Jessica S. Burbridge, Gorilla Doctors
Page 21: wolves © Lori Labrecque/shutterstock, elephants © gnomeandi/shutterstock, giraffes © Claudia Otte/shutterstock, bears © Sergey Krasnoshchokov/shutterstock

Page 21: (cont.) kangaroos © K.A. Willis/shutterstock, polar bears © andamanec/shutterstock, sheep © Karel Gallas/shutterstock, terns © Sergey Uradnikov/shutterstock, hanuman langur monkeys © Karnatarka/shutterstock, cats © Orhan Cam/shutterstock, deer © MaZiKab/shutterstock, horses © Anki Hoglund/shutterstock
Page 22: © Pichugin Dmitry /shutterstock
Page 23: © erwinf/shutterstock
Page 24: Photo courtesy of Dawn Zimmerman, Gorilla Doctors
Page 25: © Pal Teravagimov /shutterstock
Page 26: © ValeStock /shutterstock
Page 27: © Lim Yong Hian /shutterstock
Page 28: © Anton_Ivanov /shutterstock
Page 29: © sunabesyou /shutterstock
Page 30: © Andrey_Popov /shutterstock
Page 31: © Sam Chadwick /shutterstock

The author wishes to thank her wonderful grandchildren Elizabeth, Grace, Tom and William for being her inspiration.

BBM would like to thank the American Library Association for their dedication to education and children's literacy. Please visit their website for more information about the ways libraries and librarians make the world a better place: www.ala.org. For information on programs for young adults visit www.ala.org/yalsa.

For Ruth Morris Keesling, in recognition of her work
on behalf of the critically endangered mountain gorillas.

3

Meet **Pikoe** and his mother, **Izuba.**

They are mountain gorillas, a critically endangered subspecies of the eastern gorilla species. "Endangered" means that if people don't help them, the mountain gorillas will someday disappear.

There are less than 900 mountain gorillas still living in the wild. The land they live on covers three African countries: Uganda, Rwanda and the Democratic Republic of Congo.

Mountain gorillas have very thick, long, black hair. They live in the Virunga mountains where it is cold, cloudy and misty. The long, thick hair keeps them warm and protects them.

When Pikoe was born, he was very small and helpless. He needed constant care and attention from his mother, just like you did.

7

A mountain gorilla is considered to be an adult when it is between 12 and 14 years old. Male gorillas are usually about six feet tall and weigh between 350 and 450 pounds. Female gorillas are smaller, but they are still very big!

AVERAGE
GORILLA
6 feet tall
400 pounds

Mountain gorillas live in family groups. A family group on average has 15-25 members that look for food, sleep and play together.

Because mountain gorillas are so big, they need to eat a lot! Pikoe's father, Kunga, has to eat 75 pounds of food every day.

Kunga is the leader of Pikoe's family group. He is called a "silverback" because when gorilla males get older, some of their hair turns gray– like a lot of people's hair does – except the gray is on their back instead of on their head.

Gorilla mothers need to find food every day. They can search freely when the babies are on their backs riding along. Even though mountain gorillas are very big, they eat only leaves, vines and bark, shoots and roots. They also like wild celery. Sometimes they will eat insects.

Gorilla Fun Fact

Blackberries are a special treat for mountain gorillas. Blackberries only grow at certain times of the year, high on the mountains.

Mountain gorillas start looking for food very early in the day. They forage and eat most of the morning, and then they nap in the middle of the day. After resting, they search for food again.

In the evening they gather bent vines and branches to build a nest to sleep in. The gorillas will build a new nest every night.

Mountain gorillas are an important part of life on our planet. The gorillas spread seeds in the forest for new trees to grow. They let sunlight reach the mountain floor as they move around, so more trees and plants can grow.

Why are they endangered?

The biggest reason gorillas are endangered is humans. Humans are taking up more and more land that was the natural home of mountain gorillas. Gorillas are sad that their homes are being destroyed.

Gorillas can get sick or hurt.
A group of wildlife veterinarians
called "Gorilla Doctors" are
working to make them feel
better when that happens, but
it takes time and a lot of money
to support these efforts.

Sometimes gorillas are killed or captured by hunters. Babies sometimes are taken from their mothers and sold as pets. A baby gorilla does not do well without his or her own mother. All babies need their mothers' love.

Protecting our gorilla friends.

Dr. Dian Fossey studied the mountain gorillas in Rwanda for 18 years. She recorded what she learned in a book, *Gorillas in the Mist*.

Her research and great love of the mountain gorillas have led to many other people helping protect these amazing animals. She died in 1985 and is buried in the land that she fought to keep safe for her gorilla friends.

KWELI
1975_1978

MARCHESSA
1942_1980

DIGIT
1965_1977

THANK YOU, DR. FOSSEY, FOR TEACHING THE WORLD ABOUT US.

"NYIRAMACHABELLI"
DIAN FOSSEY
1932 — 1985
NO ONE LOVED GORILLAS MORE
REST IN PEACE, DEAR FRIEND
ETERNALLY PROTECTED
IN THIS SACRED GROUND
FOR YOU ARE HOME
WHERE YOU BELONG

Dian Fossey

Today, there are groups of people all over the world who are helping the mountain gorillas. Some groups are finding ways for humans and gorillas to live near each other without hurting each other. The employees of the Dian Fossey Gorilla Fund in this photo are helping keep the gorillas in their protected forest. Others are working to protect the mountain gorillas' forest homes by stopping people from cutting down the trees. You can help protect the gorillas, too!

SAVE THE FOREST HOMES!

What can you do to **help?**

You know when there is change left over after you buy ice cream and your mom says "just keep it"? If you start saving all of those coins and dollars, you can save enough money to help take care of mountain gorillas!

An easy way to do it is to take an empty jug or jar and drop all of your change into it. You can even ask your friends and family to add to the jar whenever they can.

After you have filled the jar, give these dollars to an adult you trust and have him or her use a credit card to make a donation for that amount to one of the organizations listed on the back page of this book.

Remember, no matter where you live or what you do, whether you are 5 or 105, you can choose to help make life on our planet better. Even if you start small with the quarter that was left over when you bought a pack of gum last night, you'll be surprised how quickly you can save up enough money to help mountain gorilla families like Pikoe's.

WE CAN ALL
DO OUR PART

Here are some organizations that work to protect mountain gorillas and their habitat. We encourage you to visit their websites and see what they are doing and what you can do to help.

The Dian Fossey Gorilla Fund International
800 Cherokee Avenue, SE
Atlanta, Georgia 30315
1-800-851-0203
www.gorillafund.org

The Gorilla Doctors
www.gorilladoctors.org

The Gorilla Organization
www.Gorillas.org

Mountain Gorilla Conservation Fund
www.saveagorilla.org

Endangered Species International
www.endangeredspeciesinternational.org

The African Wildlife Foundation
www.awf.org

World Wildlife Fund
www.wwf.org

IUCN Red List of Threatened Species
www.iucnredlist.org

Fauna and Flora International
www.fauna-flora.org

The Gorilla Run – A Race to Support Gorilla Conservationism at the Calgary Zoo
www.gorillarun.com

Ape Conservation Effort
www.apeconservationeffort.org

The Leakey Foundation
www.leakeyfoundation.org

The Association of Zoos and Aquariums
www.aza.org

These zoos are actively working to make life better for gorillas and all animals. For more information visit their websites or better yet, visit their location.

The Calgary Zoo Botanical Garden and Prehistoric Park (Canada)
www.calgaryzoo.org

Columbus Zoo and Aquarium (Ohio)
www.columbuszoo.org

Denver Zoological Gardens (Colorado)
www.denverzoo.org

Oklahoma City Zoological Park
www.okczoo.com

Cleveland Metroparks Zoo
www.clemetzoo.org

Dallas Zoo
www.dallaszoo.com

Detroit Zoological Society
www.detroitzoo.org

Sedgwick County Zoo (Wichita, Kansas)
www.scz.org

Woodland Park Zoo (Seattle, Washington)
www.zoo.org

Zoo Atlanta
www.zooatlanta.org

Houston Zoo
www.houstonzoo.org

Lincoln Park Zoo (Chicago)
www.lpzoo.org

Birmingham Zoo (Alabama)
www.birminghamzoo.com

Indianapolis Zoo
www.indianapoliszoo.com

Naples Zoo at Caribbean Gardens
www.napleszoo.com

Parque Zoologico de Leon (Mexico)
www.zooleon.org.mx

The Topeka Zoo (Kansas)
www.topekazoo.org

Virginia Zoo
www.virginiazoo.org

Dickerson Park Zoo (Springfield, Missouri)
www.dickersonparkzoo.org